THE *New* **Mass** BOOK

large print

redemptorist
p u b l i c a t i o n s

The New Mass Book *(large print)*
Published by **Redemptorist Publications**
Alphonsus House, Chawton, Hampshire, GU34 3HQ
Email rp@rpbooks.co.uk, www.rpbooks.co.uk
A registered charity limited by guarantee.
Registered in England 3261721.

First published 1975
This revised edition first published September 2011.
Thirty-eighth printing September 2011.

General Editor: Denis McBride C.Ss.R.
Editors: Peter Edwards and Andrew Lyon
Design: Eliana Thompson
Artwork: Peena Lad

ISBN 978-0-85231-395-4

A CIP catalogue record for this book is available from
the British Library.

Acknowledgements: Excerpts from the English
translation of *The Roman Missal* © 2010, International
Commission on English in the Liturgy Corporation.

Concordat cum originali Jane Porter.
Imprimatur + Crispian Hollis, Bishop of Portsmouth,
15 July 2011. Permission granted for distribution
in the dioceses of Scotland.

Printed by Joseph ball (Printers) Ltd, Leicester LE2 5LQ.

The Order of Mass

THE INTRODUCTORY RITES

We come together as a worshipping community, and prepare to listen to God's Word and to celebrate the Eucharist.

All stand.
The priest comes to the altar while the Entrance Song is sung.

Sign of the Cross

All make the Sign of the Cross.

Priest In the name of the Father,
and of the Son, and of the Holy Spirit.
People **Amen.**

Greeting

The priest greets the people in one of the following ways:

The grace of our Lord Jesus Christ,
and the love of God,
and the communion of the Holy Spirit
be with you all.
or
Grace to you and peace from God our Father
and the Lord Jesus Christ.
or
The Lord be with you.
And with your spirit.

The priest may briefly introduce the Mass of the day.

Penitential Act

The priest invites the people to penitence. The Penitential Act takes one of the following forms (from time to time the blessing and sprinkling of water may take place instead):

I confess to almighty God
and to you, my brothers and sisters,
that I have greatly sinned,
in my thoughts and in my words,
in what I have done
and in what I have failed to do,

All strike their breast and say:

through my fault, through my fault,
through my most grievous fault;

therefore I ask blessed Mary ever-Virgin,
all the Angels and Saints,
and you, my brothers and sisters,
to pray for me to the Lord our God.
or
Have mercy on us, O Lord.
For we have sinned against you.

Show us, O Lord, your mercy.
And grant us your salvation.

or (using these or similar words):

You were sent to heal the contrite of heart:

Lord, have mercy. **Lord, have mercy.**
or
Kyrie, eleison.　　**Kyrie, eleison.**

You came to call sinners:

Christ, have mercy. **Christ, have mercy.**

or

Christe, eleison. **Christe, eleison.**

You are seated at the right hand
of the Father to intercede for us:

Lord, have mercy. **Lord, have mercy.**

or

Kyrie, eleison. **Kyrie, eleison.**

The absolution by the priest follows:

May almighty God have mercy on us,
forgive us our sins,
and bring us to everlasting life.
Amen.

The Kyrie, eleison (Lord, have mercy) invocations
follow, unless they have already occurred as part
of the Penitential Act.

Lord, have mercy.   **Lord, have mercy.**
Christ, have mercy.   **Christ, have mercy.**
Lord, have mercy.   **Lord, have mercy.**

or

Kyrie, eleison.   **Kyrie, eleison.**
Christe, eleison.   **Christe, eleison.**
Kyrie, eleison.   **Kyrie, eleison.**

The Gloria

On Sundays (except in Advent and Lent)
and other feast days, the Gloria is sung or said:

**Glory to God in the highest,
and on earth peace to people
of good will.**

**We praise you,
we bless you,
we adore you,
we glorify you,
we give you thanks for your great glory,
Lord God, heavenly King,
O God, almighty Father.**

**Lord Jesus Christ, Only Begotten Son,
Lord God, Lamb of God, Son of the Father,
you take away the sins of the world,
have mercy on us;
you take away the sins of the world,
receive our prayer;
you are seated at the right hand
of the Father,
have mercy on us.**

**For you alone are the Holy One,
you alone are the Lord,
you alone are the Most High,
Jesus Christ,
with the Holy Spirit,
in the glory of God the Father.
Amen.**

The Collect

Let us pray.

All pray in silence for a short while, then
the priest says the Collect, a special prayer
expressing the character of today's celebration,
at the end of which the people acclaim:

Amen.

THE LITURGY OF THE WORD

God speaks to us of redemption and salvation,
and nourishes us with God's word.

 All sit.
During the Liturgy of the Word there may be
brief periods of silence for prayerful reflection.

First Reading

At the end of the reading, the reader acclaims:

The word of the Lord.
Thanks be to God.

Psalm

The cantor or reader sings or says the Psalm, and
all make the response.

Second Reading

On Sundays and some other days there is a
second reading, at the end of which the reader
acclaims:

The word of the Lord.
Thanks be to God.

Gospel

All stand.
The Alleluia or Acclamation may be sung or said to welcome the Gospel. The deacon or priest says:

The Lord be with you.
And with your spirit.

A reading from the holy Gospel according to N.
Glory to you, O Lord.

At the end of the Gospel, the deacon or priest acclaims:

The Gospel of the Lord.
Praise to you, Lord Jesus Christ.

The Homily

All sit.
A homily is preached on all Sundays, holydays and other suitable occasions. After the homily there may be a brief period of silence for reflection.

The Profession of Faith

All stand.
The following Profession of Faith, or Creed,
is sung or said on Sundays and certain other
days. During Lent and Easter time, especially,
the Apostles' Creed may be used instead (page 11).

I believe in one God,
the Father almighty,
maker of heaven and earth,
of all things visible and invisible.

I believe in one Lord Jesus Christ,
the Only Begotten Son of God,
born of the Father before all ages.
God from God, Light from Light,
true God from true God,
begotten, not made,
consubstantial with the Father;
through him all things were made.
For us men and for our salvation
he came down from heaven,

(All bow during the next three lines)

and by the Holy Spirit
was incarnate of the Virgin Mary,
and became man.

For our sake he was crucified under Pontius
        Pilate,
he suffered death and was buried,
and rose again on the third day
in accordance with the Scriptures.
He ascended into heaven
and is seated at the right hand of the Father.
He will come again in glory
to judge the living and the dead
and his kingdom will have no end.

I believe in the Holy Spirit,
the Lord, the giver of life,
who proceeds from the Father and the Son,
who with the Father and the Son
is adored and glorified,
who has spoken through the prophets.

I believe in one, holy,
catholic and apostolic Church.
I confess one Baptism for the forgiveness of sins
and I look forward to the resurrection of the dead
and the life of the world to come.
Amen.

The Apostles' Creed
I believe in God,
the Father almighty,
Creator of heaven and earth,
and in Jesus Christ, his only Son,
our Lord,

(All bow during the next two lines)

who was conceived by the Holy Spirit,
born of the Virgin Mary,
suffered under Pontius Pilate,
was crucified, died and was buried;
he descended into hell;
on the third day he rose again from the dead;
he ascended into heaven,
and is seated at the right hand of God
the Father almighty;
from there he will come to judge the living and
the dead.
I believe in the Holy Spirit,
the holy catholic Church,
the communion of saints,
the forgiveness of sins,
the resurrection of the body,
and life everlasting. Amen.

The Prayer of the Faithful
(Bidding Prayers)

After each intention there is a pause while all pray. This time of silent prayer may be followed by the next intention, or by a response such as:

Lord, hear our prayer.

The priest concludes the biddings with a prayer.

THE LITURGY OF THE EUCHARIST

Christ said, "Do this in memory of me"; and so we come to receive in Communion his Body and Blood.

 All sit.
A hymn may be sung, and the bread and wine for the celebration are brought to the altar. The priest offers prayers of blessing. If these are said aloud, the people each time acclaim:

Blessed be God for ever.

The priest completes other personal preparatory rites, then all stand as he says:

Pray, brethren (brothers and sisters),
that my sacrifice and yours
may be acceptable to God,
the almighty Father.

**May the Lord accept the sacrifice
at your hands
for the praise and glory of his name,
for our good
and the good of all his holy Church.**

Then the priest says the Prayer over the Offerings, at the end of which the people acclaim:
Amen.

The Eucharistic Prayer

The Eucharistic Prayer is chosen from those printed on pages 23-53.

The Lord be with you.

And with your spir-it.

Lift up your hearts.

We lift them up to the Lord.

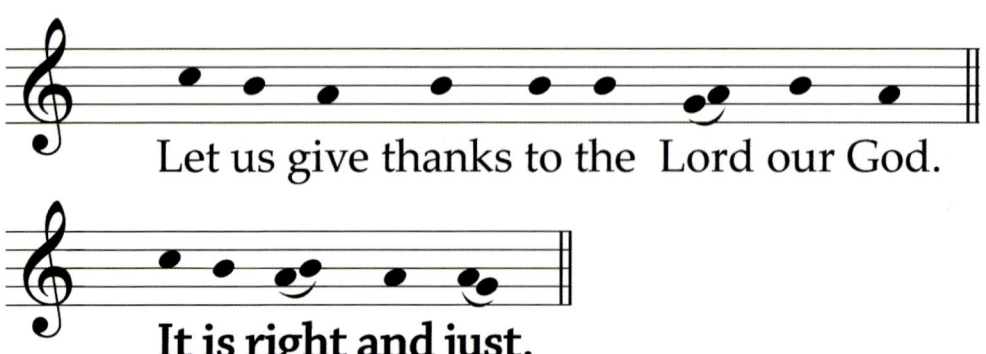

Let us give thanks to the Lord our God.

It is right and just.

The priest continues with the Preface, which varies according to the season and occasion, giving praise and thanks to God for the work of salvation. Then the priest and people join together to sing or say:

Ho-ly, Ho-ly, Ho-ly Lord God of hosts.

Hea-ven and earth are full of your glo-ry.

Ho-san-na in the high-est. Bless-ed is he

who comes in the name of the Lord.

Ho-san-na in the high-est.

The people kneel.
The priest continues with the Eucharistic Prayer.
After the words of consecration he says:

The mystery of faith.

We pro-claim your Death, O Lord,

and pro-fess your Res-ur-rec-tion

un-til you come a-gain.

or

When we eat this Bread and drink this Cup,

we pro-claim your Death, O Lord,

un-til you come a-gain.

or

Save us, Sav-iour of the world,

for by your Cross and Res-ur-rec-tion

you have set us free.

At the conclusion of the Eucharistic Prayer the priest takes the chalice and the paten with the host and, raising both, he sings or says:

Through him, and with him, and in him,
O God, almighty Father,
in the unity of the Holy Spirit,
all glory and honour is yours,
for ever and ever.
Amen.

The Communion Rite

The Lord's Prayer

All stand.

At the Saviour's command
and formed by divine teaching,
we dare to say:

**Our Father, who art in heaven,
hallowed be thy name;
thy kingdom come,
thy will be done
on earth as it is in heaven.
Give us this day our daily bread,
and forgive us our trespasses,
as we forgive those who trespass against us;
and lead us not into temptation,
but deliver us from evil.**

Deliver us, Lord, we pray, from every evil,
graciously grant peace in our days,
that, by the help of your mercy,
we may be always free from sin
and safe from all distress,
as we await the blessed hope
and the coming of our Saviour, Jesus Christ.

**For the kingdom,
the power and the glory are yours
now and for ever.**

The Peace

Lord Jesus Christ,
who said to your Apostles:
Peace I leave you, my peace I give you;
look not on our sins,
but on the faith of your Church,
and graciously grant her peace
and unity
in accordance with your will.
Who live and reign for ever and ever.
Amen.

The peace of the Lord be with you always.
And with your spirit.

Let us offer each other the sign of peace.

All offer one another the customary sign
of peace, which is an expression of peace,
communion and charity.

The Breaking of the Bread

The priest takes the host and breaks it, as the following is sung or said:

**Lamb of God, you take away the sins of the world,
have mercy on us.
Lamb of God, you take away the sins of the world,
have mercy on us.
Lamb of God, you take away the sins of the world,
grant us peace.**

Invitation to Communion

The people kneel.
The priest raises the host and says:

Behold the Lamb of God,
behold him who takes away
the sins of the world.
Blessed are those called to the supper
of the Lamb.

**Lord, I am not worthy
that you should enter under my roof,
but only say the word
and my soul shall be healed.**

After the priest has consumed the Body
and Blood of Christ, the communicants come
forward in reverent procession to receive
Communion. The Communion Antiphon may
be said or sung, or a hymn or psalm may be
sung. The priest or minister shows the host
to each of the communicants, saying:

The Body of Christ.
Amen.

When Communion is ministered under both
kinds, the minister of the chalice raises it slightly
and shows it to each of the communicants,
saying:

The Blood of Christ.
Amen.

After the distribution of Communion,
if appropriate, a silence may be observed for
a while, or a psalm or other canticle of praise
or a hymn may be sung.

Then the priest says:
Let us pray.

All stand and pray in silence. Then the priest
says the Prayer after Communion, at the end
of which the people acclaim:

Amen.

The Concluding Rites

We are sent out to fulfil in our daily lives our mission to witness to Christ in the world.

Any brief announcements now follow.
Then the dismissal takes place. This may vary according to the season and occasion.

The Lord be with you.
And with your spirit.

May almighty God bless you:
the Father, and the Son, ✚ and the Holy Spirit.
Amen.

Then the deacon or the priest says:

Go forth, the Mass is ended.

or

Go and announce the Gospel
of the Lord.

or

Go in peace, glorifying the Lord by your life.

or

Go in peace.

Thanks be to God.

A hymn may be sung.

The Eucharistic Prayers

	Page
Eucharistic Prayer I	24
Eucharistic Prayer II	30
Eucharistic Prayer III	34
Eucharistic Prayer IV	39
Eucharistic Prayer for Reconciliation I	45
Eucharistic Prayer for Reconciliation II	50

Eucharistic Prayer I
(The Roman Canon)

The Lord be with you.
And with your spirit.

Lift up your hearts.
We lift them up to the Lord.

Let us give thanks to the Lord our God.
It is right and just.

The priest continues with the Preface, which varies according to the season and occasion. The Preface concludes with the priest and people singing or saying:

**Holy, Holy, Holy Lord God of hosts.
Heaven and earth are full of your glory.
Hosanna in the highest.
Blessed is he
who comes in the name of the Lord.
Hosanna in the highest.**

 The people kneel.

To you, therefore, most merciful Father,
we make humble prayer and petition
through Jesus Christ, your Son, our Lord:
that you accept
and bless ✚ these gifts, these offerings,
these holy and unblemished sacrifices,
which we offer you firstly
for your holy catholic Church.
Be pleased to grant her peace,
to guard, unite and govern her
throughout the whole world,
together with your servant N. our Pope
and N. our Bishop,
and all those who, holding to the truth,
hand on the catholic and apostolic faith.

Remember, Lord, your servants N. and N.
and all gathered here,
whose faith and devotion are known to you.
For them, we offer you this sacrifice of praise
or they offer it for themselves
and all who are dear to them:
for the redemption of their souls,
in hope of health and well-being,
and paying their homage to you,
the eternal God, living and true.

In communion with those
whose memory we venerate,
especially the glorious ever-Virgin Mary,
Mother of our God and Lord, Jesus Christ,
* and blessed Joseph, her Spouse,
your blessed Apostles and Martyrs,
Peter and Paul, Andrew,
(James, John,
Thomas, James, Philip,
Bartholomew, Matthew,
Simon and Jude;
Linus, Cletus, Clement, Sixtus,
Cornelius, Cyprian,
Lawrence, Chrysogonus,
John and Paul,
Cosmas and Damian)
and all your Saints;
we ask that through their merits and prayers,
in all things we may be defended
by your protecting help.
(Through Christ our Lord. Amen.)

* *On certain days this text has*
special insertions which reflect the feastday.

* Therefore, Lord, we pray:
graciously accept this oblation of our service,
that of your whole family;
order our days in your peace,
and command that we be delivered
from eternal damnation
and counted among the flock
of those you have chosen.
(Through Christ our Lord. Amen.)

Be pleased, O God, we pray,
to bless, acknowledge,
and approve this offering in every respect;
make it spiritual and acceptable,
so that it may become for us
the Body and Blood of your most beloved Son,
our Lord Jesus Christ.

On the day before he was to suffer,
he took bread in his holy and venerable hands,
and with eyes raised to heaven
to you, O God, his almighty Father,
giving you thanks, he said the blessing,
broke the bread
and gave it to his disciples, saying:

Take this, all of you, and eat of it,
for this is my Body,
which will be given up for you.

* On certain days this text has
special insertions which reflect the feastday.

In a similar way, when supper was ended,
he took this precious chalice
in his holy and venerable hands,
and once more giving you thanks, he said the blessing
and gave the chalice to his disciples, saying:

Take this, all of you, and drink from it,
for this is the chalice of my Blood,
the Blood of the new and eternal covenant,
which will be poured out for you and for many
for the forgiveness of sins.

Do this in memory of me.

The mystery of faith.

**We proclaim your Death, O Lord,
and profess your Resurrection
until you come again.**

or

**When we eat this Bread and drink this Cup,
we proclaim your Death, O Lord,
until you come again.**

or

**Save us, Saviour of the world,
for by your Cross and Resurrection
you have set us free.**

Therefore, O Lord,
as we celebrate the memorial of the blessed Passion,
the Resurrection from the dead,
and the glorious Ascension into heaven
of Christ, your Son, our Lord,
we, your servants and your holy people,
offer to your glorious majesty

from the gifts that you have given us,
this pure victim,
this holy victim,
this spotless victim,
the holy Bread of eternal life
and the Chalice of everlasting salvation.

Be pleased to look upon these offerings
with a serene and kindly countenance,
and to accept them,
as once you were pleased to accept
the gifts of your servant Abel the just,
the sacrifice of Abraham, our father in faith,
and the offering of your high priest Melchizedek,
a holy sacrifice, a spotless victim.
In humble prayer we ask you, almighty God:
command that these gifts be borne
by the hands of your holy Angel
to your altar on high
in the sight of your divine majesty,
so that all of us, who through this
participation at the altar
receive the most holy Body and Blood of your Son,
may be filled with every grace and heavenly blessing.
(Through Christ our Lord. Amen.)

Remember also, Lord, your servants N. and N.,
who have gone before us with the sign of faith
and rest in the sleep of peace.

Grant them, O Lord, we pray,
and all who sleep in Christ,
a place of refreshment, light and peace.
(Through Christ our Lord. Amen.)
To us, also, your servants, who, though sinners,
hope in your abundant mercies,
graciously grant some share

and fellowship with your holy Apostles and
Martyrs:
with John the Baptist, Stephen,
Matthias, Barnabas,
(Ignatius, Alexander,
Marcellinus, Peter,
Felicity, Perpetua,
Agatha, Lucy,
Agnes, Cecilia, Anastasia)
and all your Saints;
admit us, we beseech you,
into their company,
not weighing our merits,
but granting us your pardon,
through Christ our Lord.

Through whom
you continue to make all these good things, O Lord;
you sanctify them, fill them with life,
bless them, and bestow them upon us.
Through him, and with him, and in him,
O God, almighty Father,
in the unity of the Holy Spirit,
all glory and honour is yours,
for ever and ever.
Amen.

Then follows the Communion Rite, p. 18.

Eucharistic Prayer II

This Eucharistic Prayer has its own Preface,
but it may also be used with other Prefaces.

The Lord be with you.
And with your spirit.

Lift up your hearts.
We lift them up to the Lord.

Let us give thanks to the Lord our God.
It is right and just.

It is truly right and just, our duty and our salvation,
always and everywhere to give you thanks,
Father most holy,
through your beloved Son, Jesus Christ,
your Word through whom you made all things,
whom you sent as our Saviour and Redeemer,
incarnate by the Holy Spirit and born of the Virgin.
Fulfilling your will and gaining for you a holy people,
he stretched out his hands as he endured his Passion,
so as to break the bonds of death
and manifest the resurrection.

And so, with the Angels and all the Saints
we declare your glory,
as with one voice we acclaim:

Holy, Holy, Holy Lord God of hosts.
Heaven and earth are full of your glory.
Hosanna in the highest.
Blessed is he who comes in the name
of the Lord.
Hosanna in the highest.

You are indeed Holy, O Lord,
the fount of all holiness.
Make holy, therefore, these gifts, we pray,
by sending down your Spirit upon
them like the dewfall,
so that they may become for us
the Body and ✚ Blood of our Lord
Jesus Christ.

At the time he was betrayed
and entered willingly into his Passion,
he took bread and, giving thanks, broke it,
and gave it to his disciples, saying:

TAKE THIS, ALL OF YOU, AND EAT OF IT,
FOR THIS IS MY BODY,
WHICH WILL BE GIVEN UP FOR YOU.

In a similar way, when supper was ended,
he took the chalice
and, once more giving thanks,
he gave it to his disciples, saying:

TAKE THIS, ALL OF YOU, AND DRINK FROM IT,
FOR THIS IS THE CHALICE OF MY BLOOD,
THE BLOOD OF THE NEW AND ETERNAL COVENANT,
WHICH WILL BE POURED OUT FOR YOU
AND FOR MANY FOR THE FORGIVENESS OF SINS.

DO THIS IN MEMORY OF ME.

The mystery of faith.

**We proclaim your Death, O Lord,
and profess your Resurrection
until you come again.**

or

**When we eat this Bread and drink this Cup,
we proclaim your Death, O Lord,
until you come again.**

or

**Save us, Saviour of the world,
for by your Cross and Resurrection
you have set us free.**

Therefore, as we celebrate
the memorial of his Death and Resurrection,
we offer you, Lord,
the Bread of life and the Chalice of salvation,
giving thanks that you have held us worthy
to be in your presence and minister to you.
Humbly we pray
that, partaking of the Body and Blood
of Christ,
we may be gathered into one by the
Holy Spirit.

Remember, Lord, your Church,
spread throughout the world,
and bring her to the fullness of charity,
together with N. our Pope and N. our Bishop
and all the clergy.

Remember your servant N.,
whom you have called (today)
from this world to yourself.
Grant that he (she) who was united with your
Son in a death like his,
may also be one with him in his Resurrection.

Remember also our brothers and sisters
who have fallen asleep in the hope
of the resurrection,
and all who have died in your mercy:
welcome them into the light of your face.
Have mercy on us all, we pray,
that with the Blessed Virgin Mary, Mother of God,
with the blessed Apostles,
and all the Saints who have pleased you
throughout the ages,
we may merit to be coheirs to eternal life,
and may praise and glorify you
through your Son, Jesus Christ.

Through him, and with him, and in him,
O God, almighty Father,
in the unity of the Holy Spirit,
all glory and honour is yours,
for ever and ever.
Amen.

Then follows the Communion Rite, p. 18.

Eucharistic Prayer III

The Lord be with you.
And with your spirit.

Lift up your hearts.
We lift them up to the Lord.

Let us give thanks to the Lord our God.
It is right and just.

The priest continues with the Preface, which varies according to the season and occasion. The Preface concludes with the priest and people singing or saying:

Holy, Holy, Holy Lord God of hosts.
Heaven and earth are full of your glory.
Hosanna in the highest.
Blessed is he who comes in the name of the Lord.
Hosanna in the highest.

 The people kneel.

You are indeed Holy, O Lord,
and all you have created
rightly gives you praise,
for through your Son our Lord Jesus Christ,
by the power and working of the
Holy Spirit,
you give life to all things and make them holy,
and you never cease to gather a people
to yourself,
so that from the rising of the sun to its setting
a pure sacrifice may be offered to your name.

Therefore, O Lord, we humbly implore you:
by the same Spirit graciously make holy
these gifts we have brought to you
for consecration,
that they may become the Body and ✚ Blood
of your Son our Lord Jesus Christ,
at whose command we celebrate
these mysteries.

For on the night he was betrayed
he himself took bread,
and, giving you thanks, he said the blessing,
broke the bread and gave it to his disciples, saying:

Take this, all of you, and eat of it,
for this is my Body,
which will be given up for you.

In a similar way, when supper was ended,
he took the chalice,
and, giving you thanks, he said the blessing,
and gave the chalice to his disciples, saying:

Take this, all of you, and drink from it,
for this is the chalice of my Blood,
the Blood of the new and eternal covenant,
which will be poured out for you
and for many
for the forgiveness of sins.

Do this in memory of me.

The mystery of faith.

**We proclaim your Death, O Lord,
and profess your Resurrection
until you come again.**

or

**When we eat this Bread and drink this Cup,
we proclaim your Death, O Lord,
until you come again.**

or

**Save us, Saviour of the world,
for by your Cross and Resurrection
you have set us free.**

Therefore, O Lord, as we celebrate the memorial
of the saving Passion of your Son,
his wondrous Resurrection
and Ascension into heaven,
and as we look forward to his second coming,
we offer you in thanksgiving
this holy and living sacrifice.

Look, we pray, upon the oblation
of your Church
and, recognising the sacrificial Victim
by whose death
you willed to reconcile us to yourself,
grant that we, who are nourished
by the Body and Blood of your Son
and filled with his Holy Spirit,
may become one body, one spirit in Christ.
May he make of us
an eternal offering to you,
so that we may obtain an inheritance with your elect,
especially with the most Blessed Virgin Mary,
Mother of God,
with your blessed Apostles and glorious Martyrs
(with Saint N.: the Saint of the day
or Patron Saint)
and with all the Saints,
on whose constant intercession
in your presence
we rely for unfailing help.

May this Sacrifice of our reconciliation,
we pray, O Lord,
advance the peace and salvation of all the world.
Be pleased to confirm in faith and charity
your pilgrim Church on earth,
with your servant N. our Pope and N.
our Bishop,
the Order of Bishops, all the clergy,
and the entire people you have gained for your own.

Listen graciously to the prayers of this family,
whom you have summoned before you:
in your compassion, O merciful Father,
gather to yourself all your children
scattered throughout the world.

† To our departed brothers and sisters
and to all who were pleasing to you
at their passing from this life,
give kind admittance to your kingdom.
There we hope to enjoy for ever the fullness
of your glory
through Christ our Lord,
through whom you bestow on the world
all that is good. †

Through him, and with him, and in him,
O God, almighty Father,
in the unity of the Holy Spirit,
all glory and honour is yours,
for ever and ever.
Amen.

Then follows the Communion Rite, p. 18.

† Remember your servant N.
whom you have called (today)
from this world to yourself.
Grant that he (she) who was united with your Son
in a death like his,
may also be one with him in his Resurrection,
when from the earth
he will raise up in the flesh those who have died,
and transform our lowly body
after the pattern of his own glorious body.
To our departed brothers and sisters, too,
and to all who were pleasing to you at their passing
from this life,
give kind admittance to your kingdom.
There we hope to enjoy for ever
the fullness of your glory,
when you will wipe away every tear from our eyes.
For seeing you, our God, as you are,
we shall be like you for all the ages
and praise you without end,
through Christ our Lord,
through whom you bestow on the world
all that is good. †

Eucharistic Prayer IV

It is not permitted to change the Preface of this Eucharistic Prayer because of the structure of the Prayer itself, which presents a summary of the history of salvation.

The Lord be with you.
And with your spirit.

Lift up your hearts.
We lift them up to the Lord.

Let us give thanks to the Lord our God.
It is right and just.

It is truly right to give you thanks,
truly just to give you glory, Father most holy,
for you are the one God living and true,
existing before all ages and abiding
for all eternity,
dwelling in unapproachable light;
yet you, who alone are good, the source of life,
have made all that is,
so that you might fill your creatures with blessings
and bring joy to many of them
by the glory of your light.

And so, in your presence
are countless hosts of Angels,
who serve you day and night
and, gazing upon the glory of your face,
glorify you without ceasing.

With them we, too, confess your name
in exultation,
giving voice to every creature under heaven,
as we acclaim:

Holy, Holy, Holy Lord God of hosts.
Heaven and earth are full of your glory.
Hosanna in the highest.
Blessed is he who comes in the name of the Lord.
Hosanna in the highest.

 The people kneel.

We give you praise, Father most holy,
for you are great
and you have fashioned all your works
in wisdom and in love.
You formed man in your own image
and entrusted the whole world to his care,
so that in serving you alone, the Creator,
he might have dominion over all creatures.
And when through disobedience he had lost
your friendship,
you did not abandon him to the domain of death.
For you came in mercy to the aid of all,
so that those who seek might find you.
Time and again you offered them covenants
and through the prophets
taught them to look forward to salvation.

And you so loved the world, Father most holy,
that in the fullness of time
you sent your Only Begotten Son to be our Saviour.
Made incarnate by the Holy Spirit
and born of the Virgin Mary,
he shared our human nature
in all things but sin.

To the poor he proclaimed the good news
of salvation,
to prisoners, freedom,
and to the sorrowful of heart, joy.
To accomplish your plan,
he gave himself up to death,
and, rising from the dead,
he destroyed death and restored life.

And that we might live no longer for ourselves
but for him who died and rose again for us,
he sent the Holy Spirit from you, Father,
as the first fruits for those who believe,
so that, bringing to perfection
his work in the world,
he might sanctify creation to the full.

Therefore, O Lord, we pray:
may this same Holy Spirit
graciously sanctify these offerings,
that they may become
the Body and ✠ Blood of our Lord Jesus Christ
for the celebration of this great mystery,
which he himself left us
as an eternal covenant.

For when the hour had come
for him to be glorified by you, Father most holy,
having loved his own who were in the world,
he loved them to the end:
and while they were at supper,
he took bread, blessed and broke it,
and gave it to his disciples, saying:

TAKE THIS, ALL OF YOU, AND EAT OF IT,
FOR THIS IS MY BODY,
WHICH WILL BE GIVEN UP FOR YOU.

In a similar way,
taking the chalice filled with the fruit
of the vine,
he gave thanks,
and gave the chalice to his disciples, saying:

TAKE THIS, ALL OF YOU, AND DRINK FROM IT,
FOR THIS IS THE CHALICE OF MY BLOOD,
THE BLOOD OF THE NEW AND ETERNAL COVENANT,
WHICH WILL BE POURED OUT FOR YOU AND FOR MANY
FOR THE FORGIVENESS OF SINS.

DO THIS IN MEMORY OF ME.

The mystery of faith.

**We proclaim your Death, O Lord,
and profess your Resurrection
until you come again.**

or

**When we eat this Bread and drink this Cup,
we proclaim your Death, O Lord,
until you come again.**

or

**Save us, Saviour of the world,
for by your Cross and Resurrection
you have set us free.**

Therefore, O Lord,
as we now celebrate the memorial
of our redemption,
we remember Christ's Death
and his descent to the realm of the dead,
we proclaim his Resurrection
and his Ascension to your right hand,
and, as we await his coming in glory,
we offer you his Body and Blood,
the sacrifice acceptable to you
which brings salvation to the whole world.

Look, O Lord, upon the Sacrifice
which you yourself have provided for your Church,
and grant in your loving kindness
to all who partake of this one Bread and one Chalice
that, gathered into one body by the Holy Spirit,
they may truly become a living sacrifice in Christ
to the praise of your glory.

Therefore, Lord, remember now
all for whom we offer this sacrifice:
especially your servant N. our Pope,
N. our Bishop, and the whole Order of Bishops,
all the clergy,
those who take part in this offering,
those gathered here before you,
your entire people,
and all who seek you with a sincere heart.

Remember also those who have died in the peace
of your Christ and all the dead,
whose faith you alone have known.

To all of us, your children,
grant, O merciful Father,
that we may enter into a heavenly inheritance
with the Blessed Virgin Mary, Mother of God,
and with your Apostles and Saints in your kingdom.
There, with the whole of creation,
freed from the corruption of sin and death,
may we glorify you through Christ our Lord,
through whom you bestow on the world
all that is good.

Through him, and with him, and in him,
O God, almighty Father,
in the unity of the Holy Spirit,
all glory and honour is yours,
for ever and ever.
Amen.

Then follows the Communion Rite, p. 18.

Eucharistic Prayer
for Reconciliation I

Although these Eucharistic Prayers for
Reconciliation have been provided with
a proper Preface, they may also be used with
other Prefaces that refer to penance
and conversion.

The Lord be with you.
And with your spirit.

Lift up your hearts.
We lift them up to the Lord.

Let us give thanks to the Lord our God.
It is right and just.

It is truly right and just
that we should always give you thanks,
Lord, holy Father, almighty and eternal God.

For you do not cease to spur us on
to possess a more abundant life
and, being rich in mercy,
you constantly offer pardon
and call on sinners
to trust in your forgiveness alone.

Never did you turn away from us,
and, though time and again
we have broken your covenant,
you have bound the human family to yourself
through Jesus your Son, our Redeemer,
with a new bond of love so tight
that it can never be undone.

Even now you set before your people
a time of grace and reconciliation,
and, as they turn back to you in spirit,
you grant them hope in Christ Jesus
and a desire to be of service to all,
while they entrust themselves
more fully to the Holy Spirit.

And so, filled with wonder,
we extol the power of your love,
and, proclaiming our joy
at the salvation that comes from you,
we join in the heavenly hymn of countless hosts,
as without end we acclaim:

Holy, Holy, Holy Lord God of hosts.
Heaven and earth are full of your glory.
Hosanna in the highest.
Blessed is he who comes in the name
of the Lord.
Hosanna in the highest.

 The people kneel.

You are indeed Holy, O Lord,
and from the world's beginning
are ceaselessly at work,
so that the human race may become holy,
just as you yourself are holy.
Look, we pray, upon your people's offerings
and pour out on them the power
of your Spirit,
that they may become the Body and ✠ Blood
of your beloved Son, Jesus Christ,
in whom we, too, are your sons and daughters.
Indeed, though we once were lost

and could not approach you,
you loved us with the greatest love:
for your Son, who alone is just,
handed himself over to death,
and did not disdain to be nailed for our sake
to the wood of the Cross.

But before his arms were outstretched between
heaven and earth,
to become the lasting sign of your covenant,
he desired to celebrate the Passover with his
disciples.

As he ate with them,
he took bread
and, giving you thanks, he said the blessing,
broke the bread and gave it to them, saying:

TAKE THIS, ALL OF YOU, AND EAT OF IT,
FOR THIS IS MY BODY,
WHICH WILL BE GIVEN UP FOR YOU.

In a similar way, when supper was ended,
knowing that he was about to reconcile all things
in himself
through his Blood to be shed on the Cross,
he took the chalice, filled with the
fruit of the vine,
and once more giving you thanks,
handed the chalice to his disciples, saying:

TAKE THIS, ALL OF YOU, AND DRINK FROM IT,
FOR THIS IS THE CHALICE OF MY BLOOD,
THE BLOOD OF THE NEW AND ETERNAL COVENANT,
WHICH WILL BE POURED OUT FOR YOU AND FOR MANY
FOR THE FORGIVENESS OF SINS.

DO THIS IN MEMORY OF ME.

The mystery of faith.

**We proclaim your Death, O Lord,
and profess your Resurrection
until you come again.**

or

**When we eat this Bread and drink this Cup,
we proclaim your Death, O Lord,
until you come again.**

or

**Save us, Saviour of the world,
for by your Cross and Resurrection
you have set us free.**

Therefore, as we celebrate
the memorial of your Son Jesus Christ,
who is our Passover and our surest peace,
we celebrate his Death and Resurrection
from the dead,
and looking forward to his blessed Coming,
we offer you, who are our faithful and merciful God,
this sacrificial Victim
who reconciles to you the human race.

Look kindly, most compassionate Father,
on those you unite to yourself
by the Sacrifice of your Son,
and grant that, by the power of the Holy Spirit,
as they partake of this one Bread
and one Chalice,
they may be gathered into one Body in Christ,
who heals every division.

Be pleased to keep us always
in communion of mind and heart,
together with N. our Pope and N. our Bishop.
Help us to work together
for the coming of your Kingdom,
until the hour when we stand before you,
Saints among the Saints in the halls of heaven,
with the Blessed Virgin Mary, Mother of God,
the blessed Apostles and all the Saints,
and with our deceased brothers and sisters,
whom we humbly commend to your mercy.

Then, freed at last from the wound of corruption
and made fully into a new creation,
we shall sing to you with gladness
the thanksgiving of Christ,
who lives for all eternity.

Through him, and with him, and in him,
O God, almighty Father,
in the unity of the Holy Spirit,
all glory and honour is yours,
for ever and ever.
Amen.

Then follows the Communion Rite, p. 18.

Eucharistic Prayer
for Reconciliation II

The Lord be with you.
And with your spirit.

Lift up your hearts.
We lift them up to the Lord.

Let us give thanks to the Lord our God.
It is right and just.

It is truly right and just
that we should give you thanks and praise,
O God, almighty Father,
for all you do in this world,
through our Lord Jesus Christ.

For though the human race
is divided by dissension and discord,
yet we know that by testing us
you change our hearts
to prepare them for reconciliation.

Even more, by your Spirit you move human hearts
that enemies may speak to each other again,
adversaries may join hands,
and peoples seek to meet together.

By the working of your power
it comes about, O Lord,
that hatred is overcome by love,
revenge gives way to forgiveness,
and discord is changed to mutual respect.

Therefore, as we give you ceaseless thanks
with the choirs of heaven,
we cry out to your majesty on earth,
and without end we acclaim:

Holy, Holy, Holy Lord God of hosts.
Heaven and earth are full of your glory.
Hosanna in the highest.
Blessed is he who comes in the name
of the Lord.
Hosanna in the highest.

 The people kneel.

You, therefore, almighty Father,
we bless through Jesus Christ your Son,
who comes in your name.
He himself is the Word that brings salvation,
the hand you extend to sinners,
the way by which your peace is offered to us.
When we ourselves had turned away from you
on account of our sins,
you brought us back to be reconciled, O Lord,
so that, converted at last to you,
we might love one another
through your Son,
whom for our sake you handed over to death.
And now, celebrating the reconciliation
Christ has brought us,
we entreat you:
sanctify these gifts by the outpouring
of your Spirit,
that they may become the Body and ✚ Blood
of your Son,
whose command we fulfil
when we celebrate these mysteries.
For when about to give his life to set us free,
as he reclined at supper,
he himself took bread into his hands,
and, giving you thanks, he said the blessing,
broke the bread and gave it to his disciples, saying:

TAKE THIS, ALL OF YOU, AND EAT OF IT,
FOR THIS IS MY BODY,
WHICH WILL BE GIVEN UP FOR YOU.

In a similar way, on that same evening,
he took the chalice of blessing in his hands,
confessing your mercy,
and gave the chalice to his disciples, saying:

TAKE THIS, ALL OF YOU, AND DRINK FROM IT,
FOR THIS IS THE CHALICE OF MY BLOOD,
THE BLOOD OF THE NEW AND ETERNAL COVENANT,
WHICH WILL BE POURED OUT FOR YOU AND FOR MANY
FOR THE FORGIVENESS OF SINS.

DO THIS IN MEMORY OF ME.

The mystery of faith.

**We proclaim your Death, O Lord,
and profess your Resurrection
until you come again.**

or

**When we eat this Bread and drink this Cup,
we proclaim your Death, O Lord,
until you come again.**

or

**Save us, Saviour of the world,
for by your Cross and Resurrection
you have set us free.**

Celebrating, therefore, the memorial
of the Death and Resurrection of your Son,
who left us this pledge of his love,
we offer you what you have bestowed on us,
the Sacrifice of perfect reconciliation.

Holy Father, we humbly beseech you
to accept us also, together with your Son,
and in this saving banquet
graciously to endow us with his very Spirit,
who takes away everything
that estranges us from one another.

May he make your Church a sign of unity
and an instrument of your peace
among all people
and may he keep us in communion
with N. our Pope and N. our Bishop
and all the Bishops
and your entire people.

Just as you have gathered us now
at the table of your Son,
so also bring us together,
with the glorious Virgin Mary, Mother of God,
with your blessed Apostles and all the Saints,
with our brothers and sisters
and those of every race and tongue
who have died in your friendship.
Bring us to share with them
the unending banquet of unity
in a new heaven and a new earth,
where the fullness of your peace will shine forth
in Christ Jesus our Lord.

Through him, and with him, and in him,
O God, almighty Father,
in the unity of the Holy Spirit,
all glory and honour is yours,
for ever and ever.
Amen.

Then follows the Communion Rite, p. 18.

Gloria

Gloria in excelsis Deo
et in terra pax hominibus bonae voluntatis.
Laudamus te,
benedicimus te,
adoramus te,
glorificamus te,
gratias agimus tibi propter magnam
gloriam tuam,
Domine Deus, Rex caelestis,
Deus Pater omnipotens.
Domine Fili Unigenite, Iesu Christe,
Domine Deus, Agnus Dei, Filius Patris,
qui tollis peccata mundi, miserere nobis;
qui tollis peccata mundi, suscipe deprecationem
nostram.
Qui sedes ad dexteram Patris, miserere nobis.
Quoniam tu solus Sanctus, tu solus Dominus,
tu solus Altissimus,
Iesu Christe, cum Sancto Spiritu:
in gloria Dei Patris.
Amen.

Credo

Credo in unum Deum,
Patrem omnipotentem,
factorem caeli et terrae,
visibilium omnium et invisibilium.
Et in unum Dominum Iesum Christum,
Filium Dei Unigenitum,
et ex Patre natum ante omnia saecula.
Deum de Deo, lumen de lumine,
Deum verum de Deo vero,
genitum, non factum, consubstantialem Patri:
per quem omnia facta sunt.
Qui propter nos homines et propter nostram
Salutem
descendit de caelis.
Et incarnatus est de Spiritu Sancto
ex Maria Virgine, et homo factus est.
Crucifixus etiam pro nobis sub Pontio Pilato;
passus et sepultus est,
et resurrexit tertia die, secundum Scripturas,
et ascendit in caelum, sedet ad dexteram Patris.
Et iterum venturus est cum gloria,
iudicare vivos et mortuos,
cuius regni non erit finis.
Et in Spiritum Sanctum, Dominum et vivificantem:
qui ex Patre Filioque procedit.
Qui cum Patre et Filio simul adoratur et
conglorificatur:
qui locutus est per prophetas.
Et unam, sanctam, catholicam et apostolicam
Ecclesiam.
Confiteor unum baptisma in remissionem
peccatorum.
Et exspecto resurrectionem mortuorum,
et vitam venturi saeculi. Amen.

Sanctus

Sanctus, Sanctus, Sanctus Dominus Deus Sabaoth.
Pleni sunt caeli et terra gloria tua.
Hosanna in excelsis.
Benedictus qui venit in nomine Domini.
Hosanna in excelsis.

Pater Noster

Pater noster, qui es in caelis:
sanctificetur nomen tuum;
adveniat regnum tuum;
fiat voluntas tua, sicut in caelo, et in terra.
Panem nostrum cotidianum da nobis hodie;
et dimitte nobis debita nostra,
sicut et nos dimittimus debitoribus nostris;
et ne nos inducas in tentationem;
sed libera nos a malo.

Agnus Dei

Agnus Dei, qui tollis peccata mundi:
miserere nobis.
Agnus Dei, qui tollis peccata mundi:
miserere nobis.
Agnus Dei, qui tollis peccata mundi:
dona nobis pacem.